Sydney Conteh is a Sierra-Leonean-born writer who moved to the United Kingdom at the age of five.

Sydney Conteh graduated from Anglia Ruskin University, Cambridge Campus with a bachelor degree in psychology.

I dedicate this book to my late Aunty Marion Clarkson and my late brother Suliman (Jalloh) Bah.

Sydney Conteh

THIS SOUL OF MINE

AUSTIN MACAULEY PUBLISHERS™

LONDON • CAMBRIDGE • NEW YORK • SHARJAH

A CIP catalogue record for this title is available from the British Library.

ISBN 9781398435575 (Paperback)
ISBN 9781398435582 (ePub e-book)

www.austinmacauley.com

First Published 2023
Austin Macauley Publishers Ltd®
1 Canada Square
Canary Wharf
London
E14 5AA

I would like to thank Cambridge and Coleridge Athletics Club (Sprints group), Cambridgeshire, for creating a safe place for me to assemble the collections of poems together.

I would also like to send my appreciation to Anglia Ruskin University and the associated faculties, for giving this insight into psychology, and how to implement the principles learned during my time studying.

Lastly, I would like to thank my family and friends for supporting me through the process of writing a poetry book.

This soul of mine has been broken,
Broken by demons disguised as angels.
You can still see the scars they caused.
This soul of mine has climbed mountains,
But at times struggles to walk through molehills.
This soul of mine
Has disposed of many people.
It is scared to still control its actions.

This soul of mine has had malfunctions.
Demon claws have caused the brain to go numb,
Causing times where it knows nothing
Or has nothing
But its shadow
Shadows are a distant friend
Pushing you away
While forever being part of you.

This soul of mine is a blade provider,
Giving people the weapon that may damage it
My heart is filled with emotions and painful experiences.
This soul of mine
Is hoping the receiver will treat it with kindness and love
Hoping, just hoping.

This soul of mine is mine
Is not perfect
More complicated than any mind can comprehend
More than I can comprehend
So this is my soul. What's yours?

Chapter 1
Under the Waves

Sometimes, life is an ocean.

We are swimming.

Every time we move, we are overcast by troubles.

Breathing is meant to be easy

When surrounded by self-hate water that others make or

You make like secreting it from your pores

Breathing is the last thing we want to do

But still, our inner voice says breath

Says the waves will end

Says soon we will have the strength to swim to the surface

So breathe because this is the only life you will get.

It is precious and beautiful.

We are precious and beautiful.

It is said water distorts vision.

We can be under the waves for so long that we forget how

Beautiful we are.

Sometimes, we just need to endure life's turbulent waves

To notice how beautiful we are.

When the Sunset Comes

When the sun sets,
The ground metamorphoses to show demons
The darkness housing claws and teeth
Only broken by hopeful streetlights.

When the mind sets,
Neurons metamorphoses,
Revealing all the demons' depression held back
Only broken by the love of family and friends.

I do not like sunsets.
I know they are inevitable
So I have learnt to cherish all the sunlight
Because I do not know when the darkness will return.

Last Prayer

Hi there,
The cuts on your wrist tell me that you want to break free.
Your mind chains you.
This grey matter has consumed you
Makes you think that these grey skies matter.
The clouds will rain soon.
You are just like many flowers in the meadow waiting to
Bloom
But your mind has stopped you from seeing your colours.

A rainbow of hope
You, oh, you travelling soul
Trying to find a place to call home
Cracked mirror in the funhouse that is life
You are not lost.
You haven't opened your eyes.
It is easy to seem lost
When depression has blinded you
When trauma has scared your pupils
Leaving you only seeing shadows
So you hide, but these shadows are angels.
You are not cracked.

You have fault lines.
Some people are better at hiding them.

So let us bow our heads
If you believe in a god,
Then say his names.
I will say: my friends and family, as they are the gods I follow
Let us say our last prayer
That we don't let our brain trap us without fighting
That we sing
Music is freedom personified
And dance is our bodies celebrating its liberty.
Lastly, I know there may be a storm in your heart
But they are always serenity
As long as that is present,
You will never walk alone.

Paper Prison

The lines hold back grey-matter bars of hate.
Paragraphs are the chains that hold them back.
Vowel and consonants
Create a multitude of traps,
Combining to create miracles
And this pen is the warden that controls it all
All to manage the dark side of myself
It has self-harm hands
You can see the bruises it causes.
Insecure legs,
Keeping me stuck
Unmoved, legs saying you are not good enough.
This pen created a paper prison
And these words are my depression's jail sentence.

Chasm

If I can have a superpower,
I will have super strength.
Why? Because
Body moves forwards
While the mind is having a gated protest.
Body speaks words
That the mind is foreign to.
My body learnt the words from others
Like an instructional guide on how to operate through life.

Body sleeps
While the mind is racing with thoughts.
Body is awake
While the mind is suppressed.
My mind and body
Are a bad divorced couple
Who don't see they are the missing piece in their life
Keeping each other at arm's distance
Like a hedgehog
Who craves warmth on a cold winter's day
But is scared to get close
As spindles hurt

That kind of pain doesn't go away quickly.
If I can have a superpower,
I will have super strength
So I can pull back
The chasm between
My mind
And my body.
Maybe then
I will be
Considered whole.

Realising I Don't
Need You, Shadow

It's funny how you are around when I don't want you.

You are the monster under my consciousness.

I have known you far too long.

You can say we are in an abusive relationship.

You push me to the edge.

You made me question life.

You are always there even when you shouldn't

At a party

At a restaurant

With my friends

You are my ugly shadow.

So loneliness and depression

Today, I am not requesting to allow space for happiness.

I am forcing you to.

I need happiness.

I know you will always be a part of me, but will never be all
Of me.

The Things I Do Not Say

That I am scared
Scared of the present
Past
Future
I do not say
That the crippling existential thought of life is easy
It flows smoothly as whisky through my mind.

I do not say
That behind my stubbornness
Sometimes stupid stubbornness
Keep me moving forward when my body wants to stop
Sometimes my stubbornness is my saving grace.
Sometimes my stubbornness is my inner child,
Holding on to my dreams, even when my body cannot see
them.

I do not say 'thank you' enough.
Every morning, I dislike the person that contorts himself out
Of bed.
I need to thank him more.
Thank you for finding the strength to live every day.

I do not say
'I love you' enough to see my reflection in the mirror.
Maybe that's why I sometimes seek attention from others.
Maybe that's why I keep trying to fill a hole that I keep
Digging.
I try filling it with forced words, fished from the mouths of
others
But that hole will never be filled unless I say to myself, "I love
you."

I do not say that I need help.
I have beaten myself up so much that my cuts are becoming
Visible for the world to see.
I do not say I am an introvert with an identity crisis
Like being an extrovert is heavenly.

I do not say sometimes I duel on my pain.
It's easy to duel on pain even if it's gone.
But life is pain.
The pursuit of happiness can be a pain.
Isn't that the paradox of life?

So instead of saying these things,
I will write it on my skin and show it in my actions.
I will only show it to the few.
So, though the words may not touch my tongue,
As it will burn it,
You will see the things I do not say in my skin and actions.

Continental Drift (Inspired By The Story of a Personal Friend)

(Disclaimer: contains the theme of suicide. If you are going through this, please seek professional help. Services from the UK will be noted at the bottom of this poem.)

The first time you think of suicide,
You may have a smile on your face, but inside, you will be crying out.
When you are rock-bottom, the worst thing to say is: the only
Way is up
That never helps
Looking up reminds you of how much work you have to do.
Looking down at the thought of suicide makes life so easy.
If you are reading this and you know someone who has depression,
Who is in a peaceful place in their life,
Do not be worried about them
But be aware of how easy it for them to fall into pieces.

See, depression is like tectonic plates.
Sometimes they split, revealing all your insecurities that lay in your mantle.

Sometimes your self-esteem is like a continental plate.
Then the oceanic plate of trauma, heartache and grief
Drives deep under your self-esteem
You erupt
You apologise for your magma verbs
You apologise for volcanic constants
As that is just depression erupting
You will apologise to the people closest to you who suffer
Because you will see the burns your depression caused on their skin.

If you are reading this and you know someone who has depression,
Who is in a peaceful place in their life,
Do not be worried about them
But be aware of how easy it is for them to fall into pieces.
This poem is to say, next time their tectonic plates open,
They may not find the strength to close the gap.
You now know the signs.

This poem is to say, they are not always fine.
Sometimes they will carry a dam behind their eyes full of tears
When that dam breaks, they will need your help.
In those times, they will not ask for help with words.
They will do it in their actions.
Their smiles and eyes will be screaming out; I need help!
So if you see the signs,
Please help them.

I Need a Translator

"Cerebro decir
Ayuda
Estoy atrapado
Yo nessito ayuda
Estoy atrapado Estoy Gritado por favor, ayuda," the body
Says.
Today is another low day.
Muscles too weak to move,
Lungs too heavy to breathe,
It's a mystery.
Why am I like this?
My body and mind are speaking two languages.
Yo nessito una traductor
Is it you?

I Know it Hurts

I know it hurts.
He said those words that felt like an atomic bomb to your
Self-esteem.
He made you feel special
Put a throne beneath you and lifted you to the heavens
Now he is watching you fall.
You think to yourself,
Was it my fault?
Was my love not enough to fill his cup?
Did I leave him half-full?
Take the good,
Use it, make yourself a throne
Because you are a queen.
Leave the bad.
Use it as a reminder as what love is not.

I know it hurts; she was the one.
You placed her on your fondest memories.
Been dating for so long,
You were thinking of saying those four beautiful words.
Now she is gone, and your heart is wanting something that is
already gone.

You make a brave face in public,
But inside, there is a dam waiting to break.
One more absent thought of her, it will break,
Flooding the floor with sorrow
You reason, these tears are not worth spilling.
Harden your shell
So no one sees how your beautiful meadow
Has been affected by tornado words: "It's over.
It's not you; it's me."

Here is the truth
Do not be afraid to cry.
Crying is your body cleansing itself,
Leaving space for new love.
Take the good,
Put them in your fondest memories.
Take the bad,
Use them as a reminder of what love is not.
Remember the heart can break easily,
But it always heals.

When Love Goes

I gave you my power,
Opened my heart,
It flowed out of me,
Leaving me defenceless.
You disregarded me
Let my power evaporate into dust,
Leaving me weak and heartbroken.
I gave you my power,
And you wasted it.
Look at me now.
I am a stronger person.

Kami and Bachi

Definitions:
Kami: (Noun)
god; deity; divinity; spirit.

Bachi : (Noun)
(divine) punishment; curse; retribution

Bachi ga ataru: Something bad will happen to you if your actions are malicious.

It looks like me, but it is not.
The same face moulded into something I don't even
Recognise.
The mirror labels me *kami*
As I am divine in my best days
Treating my words as if they were medicine
Choosing to heal people
Choosing to heal myself *kami*
Demon resides within
Some times
Most times
All the time I say,

I say, *"Bachi ga ataru,"* and
Predict the future and perform my own *bachi*
I leave this body in ruins just to make it look like the distorted
View of myself

Kami are also kind
So I end up putting myself back together
While the voices in my head are saying you are due a *bachi.*
You are due a *bachi.*
You are due a *bachi.*
I say, "No,
I will decide to let my divine shine."

Just a Dream

I held you; it was just a dream.
I kissed you, just a dream
I sang to you; it was a dream
I unlocked my lungs
Said everything I held back from you, it was just a dream.
Just a dream
Hopefully, I should wake up soon.

Since you left, I have been sleepwalking, moving lips from
Strangers become your voice
Every face on TV becomes your face,
Just you
You even possess my "I love you."
Gave it to you as I thought you would be its sole owner
Now I struggle to say it
That's why love is often a distant dream
Just a dream.

Chapter 2
Wind Flyer

Let us fly.
Let us catch the wind
And just fly.
Let our souls be one with the wind.
Let us have solar-powered imaginations.
Let walls become bridges
So that nothing will be an obstacle.
Let's be truly free
Be one with the wind.

To Be A Child

To be a child
Is to be a ray of sunshine in the darkness.
To be a child
Is to be a template.
Ready to be moulded
Every day is getting better.
To be a child
Is to have a twinkle in your
eyes
Like there is a star ready to
go supernova

An uncontrollable force
How we use it is a mystery
A weapon is a weapon
Just matters how you use it.
To be a child
Is sometimes
To be trapped in an adult body
Screaming to break free
Maybe when we are old

Close to death
We release it
To remind us that life is better with
A smile
At the end of the day, we are all
Children.
We just act like it when we have
The innocence of youth
And when we have the weight of a
Life lived.
So tell me,
When did you last release your inner
Child?

Wrinkles

Someday, I am going to be a wrinkled old monster.
My eyes will fade.
A fog will eclipse it,
Limiting my vision to white.

Heart will run low
Blood will become thick
Breathing will become hard

Still I will smile.
A life filled with love and laughter
Will be worth a wrinkled body.

In This Room

Voices bounce skilfully off the walls,
Somersaulting through carefree.
The sound waves concord their way into our ears,
Childishly tickle ear follicles
Joy molecules seep through the brain,
Carving a smile on our faces

All this contained in this room.

Infinity

Say hello to infinity.
It's scary
It's like walking through a mist
That's love
It's scary
It's mysterious
And through it all, you don't know where you are going.
All you know is not knowing never felt so good.
The best part of love is that you have a partner on this journey,
So when you are lost, you have a guiding light.
Say hello to infinity.
It's your new friend.

Knat

Knat language is one of magic.

It is fantastical

Only composed of one word.

But look closely; you will see a universe.

Look closely, and you will see all the wild thoughts of Childhood

Like an uncaged curious mind tasting the sweet nectar of life.

Look closely; you will see unadulterated hope, love and Curiosity

Untouched by life and time.

The knat language is simple,

Composed of one word,

Two if you add a descriptive,

Like bird knat,

Mainly hand gestures,

As words cannot contain and express the knat language.

Knat language reminds me that age gives us wisdom

Youth gives us bravery

Bravery to just be in the moment.

I Do Not Feel Guilty

I do not feel guilty for the way my smile sculpts my face into
A masterpiece.
Say what you want; your barbed words will not erode my
Happiness.
I do not feel guilty for the way my passion is like an unending
Volcano.
A lava flows out my mouth every time I speak.

I do not feel guilty for the way I shine.
My divine is precious.
I will never feel guilty for it.

Hello Nature

Air seeps through the door,
Bouncing, hanging and slitting through my body.
I am one with nature.
I am at peace.

The sun rays touch my skin,
Revitalising every cell in my body.
I am one with nature.
I am at peace.

The air and the sun rays
Intermingle, combining to create harmony.

The sound of nature calms me.
Sound waves causing ripples into the air,
Waves that cause this body to morph
Free forming to be one with
I am one with nature.
I am at peace.

I feel the sound waves in my body
Heart beating like a great drum.

I feel the air travelling down my throat
Lungs embrace oxygen and realise toxins
I feel cells waking.
Sunlight kissing skin
Skin says, "I am ready."

I am one with nature.
I am at peace.
I am ready for the day.

The Female Sermon

If these walls could speak,
They will be singing a sermon.
Their voices will be hoarse, as their 2D voice boxes
Will 3D themselves to accommodate the power and velocity
Of this song.
The song will say,
You are beautiful.
The world will try to drown out the words.
You are beautiful.
Makeup
No makeup
Tall
Short
Teacher
Builder
Doctor
Whatever the job is, you are beautiful.

Let these words be your mirror.
Let this song reflect back all the way you shine.
Look at the words so much that they become an earworm.
Let it dive deep inside your brain.

Let it mould your personality.
Let your mind gauge the levels of your strength,
Not the funhouse mirrors you see on social media
Or in the doubtful words of others.

Let this sermon reverberate off the walls.
Let it create a throne.
You are royalty.

Living in a society where your crown will not be recognised,
You will need to stand tall.
This is a poem for every woman.
Always listen to your sermon.

Wanted

She has supernova eyes
Bursting with colour
She has a furnace heart of gold and diamond
Burns with passion and love
If you look carefully, you can see the glow in her smile.
She has a black hole mind,
Always absorbing knowledge.
Her voice makes you believe in a god
Don't mean to be cliché
There must be a god if angels like her exist.
Her wings engulf me.
I dare not get closer.
But if I don't, I fear that I may have regret in doing so.
If you find her,
Please say to her
You are now the owner of my heart.
It has your name engraved on to it,
Although maybe it will be short,
But I know the remnants of you will live on.

When a Man Says He Loves You

If a man tells, he loves you
That him fighting through so many insecurities,
You can see it through his skin
That's him making his defences paper-thin.

When a man tells you, he loves you,
His words will be heavy as gold
His words will fight up his throat
Those words will be the truest words he will ever say.

When a man tells you, he loves you,
That's him giving you his heart and a loaded gun.
He hopes you will drop the gun,
But he knows you may use the gun to break him,
Leaving him jigsawing himself together.

We, men, face so much rejection that we decide to guard our
Hearts
But when a man says he loves you,
All his defences are lowered,
So do not be a Trojan horse.
Some gates, when damaged, will take a long time to reopen.

Wings

My wings were broken,
Unable to fly.
I had to stay grounded, knowing that my wings will blossom,
That my wings will unfold, like a butterfly coming out of a
chrysalis,
Wings so big that they will cast shadows,
Shadows that I could not see or chose not to see.
Negativity can blind you from seeing the parts of you that are
Like a tranquil stream
A meadow flowering, with flowers
Not a forest fire

That is to say; we have beauty within us,
But we chose to see what is most destructive about ourselves.

Dear Future Treasure

I will store all the words you speak,
Keep them between forever and eternity
I will harmonise with your voice so that we are always in
Sync.
I will make it my mission to honour you.
We may go through war
Words of hatred will fill the air like a thick fog
So thick that we may not see our future
But we will get through it
I will wear every battle on our chest, as a reminder of all the
things we have gone through

For the times where you may have lost your confidence,
I will go to the ends of the Earth to help you find it so that
You will shine so bright that the world will look and smile.

So to the future resident of my fondest dreams,
I have not met you yet.
When we do meet,
I will give you a key and say, "This is the key to my heart.
It is yours now."

Mexican Doll

Today I saw love in a Mexican doll.
It was kind and sweet.
It gave without never asking anything in return.
It gave because it was the right thing to do.
Love is gentle, yet it can burn like a thousand suns.
Love smiles at the goodness in people's hearts.
Love holds you tightly, knowing the bad in you.
Love chooses to highlight the good.

Today I saw love in a Mexican doll.
I am grateful for the love I saw.

Chapter 3
Riding the Wave

Sometimes, life's troubles are not strong enough to submerge
You
Yet, life's pleasures are not strong enough to lift you.
You are just there riding the waves.

The Pen

The pen is the bridge between the mind and the paper
As we write
It transfers emotions to words,
Leaving the body without pain
Even just for a second.

Learning to Love

I am still learning to love.
I am still trying to be kind, to love
Kind to myself
I carry the sword on the left hand,
Cutting myself with razor-blade words
Carry a plaster on the right hand
Just to fix myself up again

I am still learning to be patient in love.
If love was a painting,
Well, there will be many unfinished paintings in my memory.
I am still learning to love generously
Sometimes treat love, like it's rare
Maybe that's why I don't share it

I am still learning to love with charity.
We are all cracked.
That cannot be covered up
Or not looked at
Sometimes we need to let down our ego.
I need to release my cracks
As a sign of strength

That being cracked doesn't mean you cannot be stronger.
Those cracks or flaws are a medal of valour.
Not all of us will be part of an army,
But we all have purple hearts.

Love is complicated to have.
Each part of it takes years to master,
So let us be students of love.
Love is not just romantic.
Love connects all of us,
The one thread that spans lifetimes,
So let us learn to love.

Leaf-Picking

I walk through your neuron pathways,
Skipping past myelin sheath rocks
And looking at grey matter trees
They were once so green
But now they are bare
Branches with no leaves
Some leaves carry memories.
The first 'I love you'
That reverberated in the air,
That was the best song I have ever heard.
The memory of the first time we danced,
Hands intertwined like vines on a tree,
Eyes locked onto each other,
Looking at forever,
But now they lie on the floor.
Your shaking hands cannot pick them up.

I know you feel the emotions
Must be hard
Being so happy and not knowing why
You smile at the sight of me,
Not knowing my name or why

Almost like your past life follows you
Dementia may have removed the memories,
But your roots never die
The way we made each other feel
Is still there
And all these leaves
I have kept them safe in my fondest memory

So that if dementia weakens its grip on you,
I will give them back to you
A small time to see the person I fell in love with
And if its hold tightens,
I will forge all those memories in my smile, my hugs, my kiss
So that you can see and feel all those memories.
I know it will only get worse.
Soon there will be no more leaves left at all
So I guess I have more leaf-picking to do
My inner sanctum

Here lie the remains of me
On the walls
Are the parts I disposed of
So that when they fall,
They are a gem to remember the old me
Walk through my floors
See the sides of my personality that shine
That's why I show them as colourful mosaics
So that many who dismiss me
May see it
As a shining light of what I am and who I will become
For the few who stay

Look at the cracked walls
Broken pavement
That lie there
Unfixed, hoping time will do that
That never happens
This sanctum is me
As you look at the mosaics
Acknowledge the flaws that I don't hide
As I am my strength and weakness
If I let you in,
Don't break down the pillars that I stand by
If you do,
That broken mess will take a long time to build.
So here is my sanctum
All of me
Shown bare and free to see.

This War of Mine

This war of mine is one that I am an observer
Frantically fighting, but this war affects me insidiously
This war places me to the point of destruction
Malfunction of my Neurosoup
Sometimes it feels like my body controls me,
Rather than me controlling my body
My body is in a long-term civil war
Between my mental health and my happiness
The anxiety of life ever-present
Never pleasant
Resentment may be easy to feel towards this body.

My face is a fake peace treaty
Or a warning
Do not enter
Unless you want to fuel the battle inside me
I smile and say, "I am good."
Mostly the truth, but behind my words,
Insecurities are having an uprising.
I have become so used to them that it is desensitising.
They are two sides of this war;
My mental health is on one side

My pride, happiness and family on the other side
My dreams are the predictors of this war
As long as my dreams reside in the stars,
I do not fear falling into the abyss of my mind
Knowing if I do fall, I will rise again.

This war of mine is yours too.
We need allies to win this war, as no war is won alone.
Happiness never comes from solitude,
Though complete victory is impossible
We can make the chains that try to hold us back,
A small part of the person we are
So when you see a friend, show them your scars
And say, "Let's win this war together."

Teaching Myself to Love

I do not know how to love.
I overthink.
My head is a scrabble game
With too many letters
With too many answers
In the end, I never form a word I like,
But my move has already ended,
So I am just there with a word that is never said.
I give that word so much weight; it becomes an anchor from
My past

When I do not overthink,
I grab at anything I see, meaning I never let things develop
If relationships are photos,
Then I have a photo album filled with blurred photographs.

I am learning to love,
Learning to take it slow,
Learning to stay in the present,
Someday, I will look back and be proud of what I Learnt.

Sacrificing to My Alter

Give me a sweet kind of poem
The type of poem that envisages a beautiful, vibrant meadow
The type of poem makes you forget about your mortality,
Balancing on a knife-edge every day
Give me sunshine and rainbow poems
All these I say to myself when I am low
That is to say that my mental health creates a subgenre of
Poetry
Poetry that is like emotional bleeding

This poem is an altar.
I have sacrificed my demons in these words
So that the masses are able to see sunshine and rainbow poems
The few will see all the sacrificed demons

This book carries so many demons.
I fear if I show, you may run
This alter
This book
This poem
My poems are at times,
The only thing keeping these demons back

So when I say a love poem,

Know that I had to bleed out the self-hate within me,

To tell it

When I say a poem of action,

Know that I have to bleed out the chains of insecurity that

Hold me back

Every time you hear my meadow poems,

Just know the bleeding needed to show it.

The Act of Letting Go

I held my heart to you
Dug up all my essence to give it to you
My **love**
I made our love sacred
You with a flaming heart
But with a mellow mind

That is to say; you burn with a passion that I radiate through
You
Your collected mind reminds me that I deserve to be loved
But now we are two drifting continents that were once so
Close
Now **I must** amplify our conversations to hear you
I often now say, must I reply to all the memories we had
I collected them and made them into a movie.
I **let** that movie play, as our time will always play through my
Mind
The meaning I will give **You**
Will constantly change
As the river of time will erode me and evolve me
I take pleasure that our movie will always make me smile.
So I say,

Go

I know that our time has come, but thank you for opening up
The parts of me that I closed
You showed me that I could love the monsters I locked inside,
Embrace them and with a smile, let them go
So I held my heart to you
Now it is time to give it to someone else.

Therapy

At times, my words are clumsy.
They stutter, and they stumble at the sight of a pretty face.
They have a balloon-like ego when covered with insecurities.
When it bursts, I am left picking up the piece of my
Self-esteem
When my words are pure and true,
They are vulnerable, but they are free.
They sing and dance when the pen kisses the paper,
Knowing paper never rejects love, but listens to it
The paper never judges my mental-health problems.
Use me instead of a fist
Use me; I will never hurt you.

Lessons I Learnt from Life

One, black is beautiful.
Two, African is beautiful.
I have both, so I am overflowing with beauty.
Three, friends hold value in your heart.
So choose your friends wisely,
As they can become your extended family.
Problems always arise if you choose wrongly.
Problems are solved when you are found and helped by true
Friends.

Four, there are days when you will look in the mirror and say,
We are broken
We are scarred
But like fine art, where its imperfections add to its beauty,
We are not meant to be perfect
Take your broken heart and scars
Realise that they are a small part of the masterpiece you are.
Five, never let others value your worth.
Six, never let others determine your happiness.

Seven, the ending of aspects of your life is the start of
Something better

Eight, the ending of a dream means it has become a reality.

Dream again

Always dream

Never give up on your dreams.

Life is too short not to dream about all the things you can
Become

Lastly, let the words 'I am beautiful' to be a permanent
Resident in your mouth

The world can say it to you, and it will mean nothing.

Say it to yourself, and you will always find happiness.

Completing the Puzzle of Life

I know you feel like a jigsaw puzzle with many missing
Pieces.
Your brain keeps screaming; it needs a muzzle.
All you need is silence,
Silence to piece back together with your funhouse life.
Everywhere we go, everything is distorted.
'Hello' becomes a detailed critique of you.
When stripped bare, you can see nothing good.
You create a mask to change your mood
That never works
Even chameleons have their true colours.

Funhouse mirrors do not hold the correct puzzle pieces,
So try this;
Go crazy and break all your mirrors,
As they are not your true reflection,
More of a misdirection only showing a perceived affliction.

I know your mind is strong,
So break your mental funhouse, just to find new puzzle pieces,
The pieces that fit you perfectly
You will feel complete.

Feeling complete is seeing yourself not through distorted
Eyes, but in the reflection of your deeds
Observe the moon crescent smiles you cause; they care more
About you
Than funhouse mirrors

So fight one more day.
You still got more smiles to create
You still have more puzzle pieces to find.
Soon you will feel whole.

Looking in The Mirror

I hate you sometimes.
I hate how you always search for love,
But always in the places it does not exist
Just to *papier mache* your face to the world
So that the world sees you are searching for love,
Yet you do not feel it
I get it; I do not resent your reason.
Fake love has sent you to prison for the crime of innocence
You're scared
You cannot discriminate in the face of true love anymore.

I hate that you think you can not
I hate that you think that your mental mould is set
I hate that you think your feet are not on a free road,
But train rails
You are scared to derail.

Truth is the truth.
The pavement in the pavement
Your feet have been walking this whole time
Sometimes you suffer from life dysmorphia.
You do not notice the love that is all around you.

Just stop

Blink

Allow yourself to notice all the love you have.

I am not saying this to lie

Because I am you,

You are looking in the mirror

Choosing to look at the pieces of you that are not broken

After I have spoken

After I have manifested all the words,

My lungs held for so long

After I have erupted all my words

Leave them in this room,

So you can see them every time you enter

Listen to me more.

Listen on the days I seem like a metaphor.

Listen when I am a tiny light in the corner of the mirror.

Let that light grow.

Let that light engulf the whole mirror

So all you see is light

Because you cannot see yourself in a dark room.

Bee Problem

Today, a bee dug into my brain
Stinger in skin
Skin-sealed pain

Bee buzzed
Knife looks good
Cut yourself

Bee buzzed
Life is worthless
Cut yourself

Bee buzzed
You are worthless
Cut yourself

Bee buzzed
Life is pain
Cut yourself

I do not get many bees anymore.
This bee is a silent voice

Easily banished by willpower
Easily silenced by my family
I remember days when I harboured hives

Millions of buzzing bees
Knife looks good
Cut yourself

Millions of buzzing bees
Life is worthless
Cut yourself

Millions of buzzing bees
You are worthless
Cut yourself
Millions of buzzing bees
Life is pain
Cut yourself.

I have learnt like bees are the foundation for life.
My bees remind me that I have work to do.
Bees remind me to look at my garden, smell the flowers
Smile and notice the best parts of me
For there to be bees, you need to have beautiful flowers.

Ingram Content Group UK Ltd.
Milton Keynes UK
UKHW010952070423
419773UK00012B/996

9 781398 435575